Dedicated to:
Ken, my ridiculously good looking husband.
You awakened the song in my heart. I love you.
And for my grandma, Gracie Cooper
You gave me wings to fly and consistent love.
More than words...
                    - Alisha

For my daughter Madison   - Amy

"For I know the plans I have for you," says the Lord,
"plans to prosper you and not to harm you,
plans to give you hope and a future."
Jeremiah 29:11

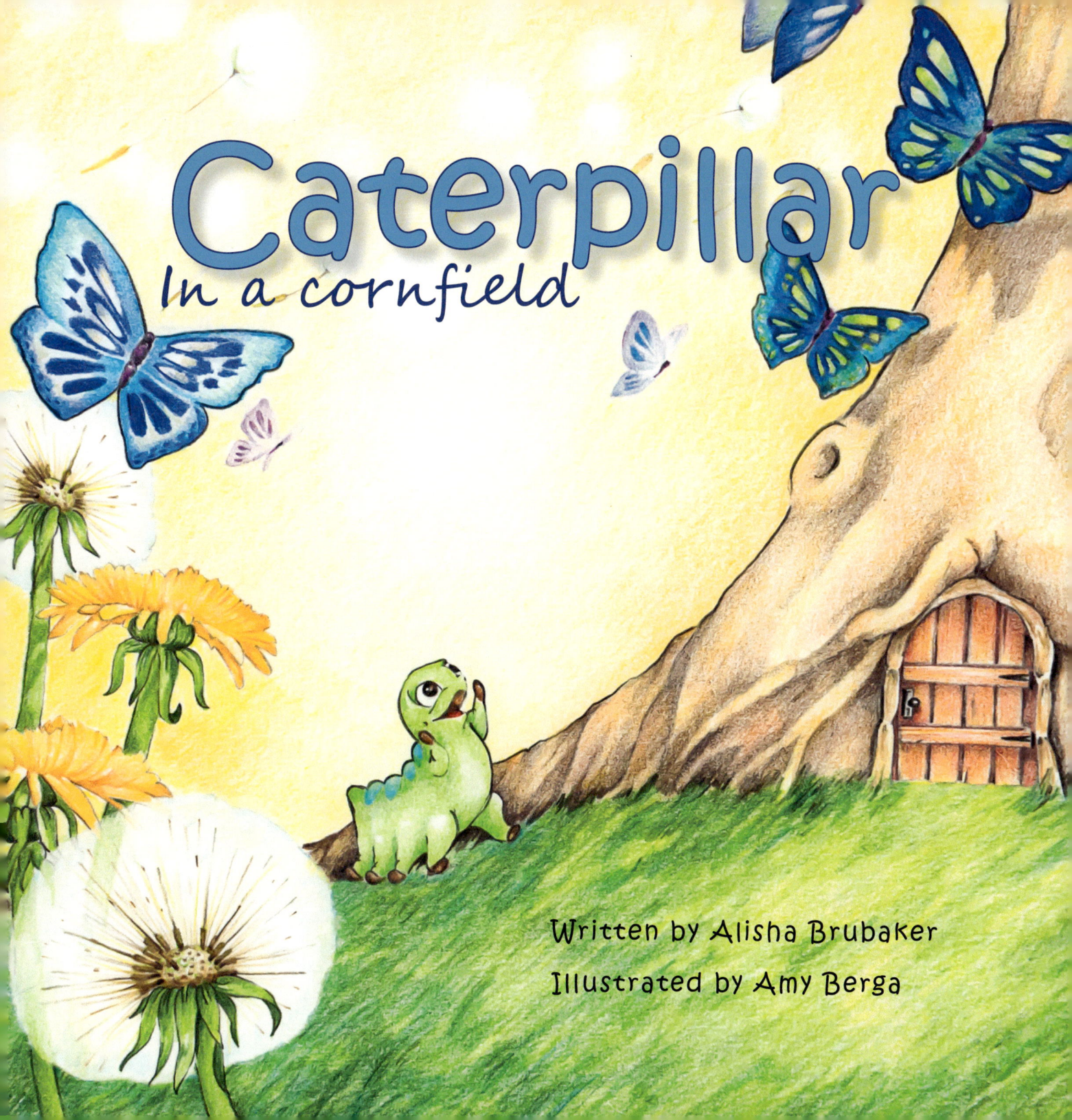

Fuzzy and green with little blue dots,
Caterpillar says, "I love to take walks!

It's fun to do and it helps me grow strong.
I just wish going places didn't take so long."

As he inched along, shaded from the sun,

He said to himself, "Climbing a cornstalk would be fun."

As he drew close, he saw a lady bug start to climb.

"Why, I've arrived here just in time."

"Hello, Lady Bug!
I couldn't help but see
that you're sprinkled with dots just like me.
You're red with black dots and I'm green with blue.
I'm just so happy that I'm meeting you."

Lady Bug turned and saw it was true.
Her dots were black and his were blue.
"There are leaves at the top that are juicy, you see.
Would you like to climb to the top with me?"

Caterpillar nodded and said with a grin,
"I love that I've just made a new friend."
Caterpillar inched and Lady Bug tip-toed
when they came upon an ant with a heavy load.

Ant was plain black with no colored dots,
and the corn he carried made him struggle a lot.
"No time for fun. No time to take walks.
I'm not like you with your colored dots.
I work all day to collect kernels of corn;
each day is the same." he said quite forlorn.

"But you're very strong and really fast.
You make quick work of your every-day task."

Ant said, "It's true, I get quite a lot done.
I like to be out working in the sun,
and I'm stronger than most even without colored dots.
Hey, you made me feel better; thanks, thanks a lot!"
Lady Bug tip-toed to let Ant pass,
and he carried on with his day-to-day task.

Inching along and tip-toeing together,

the climb to the top seemed to take forever.

Lady Bug said, "You're only a little like me.

The colored dots we have in common are all that I see.

You inch along at a very slow pace.

I could win if this were a race."

Caterpillar sighed because he knew it was true,
but God made him this way, so what could he do?

"God made you to fly, and I inch along,
but God made me this way so I could grow strong.
There's something more God made me for.
I want to be ready for what He has in store.
So every day I walk, inch, and climb
until the day comes when He says,
'It's time.'"

"What does He have in store for you
with your fuzzy green body with spots that are blue?
You can't fly like me; you're not fast like Ant.
God surely can't use you...No, no He can't."

"He has a plan. I know it's true,
but you're right, I don't know what He'll do.
I know He'll do something. It will be grand,
for everyone He has a plan."

They reached the top and decided to rest,
and they started to munch on the leaves that were best.
The caterpillar yawned, "Ahh...I think it's time.
God wants me to make a bed
that's all mine."

"You can't, not here, this isn't your home.
Am I to climb down without you? Alone?"

"I know you don't like it, but I know it's true.
There is something wonderful He's about to do."

Like a head-to-toe sleeping bag he zipped himself up, and Lady Bug turned away with a "Huff!"

"Fuzzy, green and sprinkled with dots;
when he wakes up I'm going to laugh at him a lot.
He can't fly, and he's slow as he inches along.
God doesn't have a plan for him; he's wrong."
Still, Lady Bug stayed by her fuzzy green friend.
"Whether he's right or wrong, he's my friend 'til the end."

A few weeks passed with Lady Bug still there.
Even Ant came by to see how they'd fared.

Out popped his head, on his face a big grin.
"Now I bet there's a race I could win!"

He came out of bed on long thin legs;

fell to his knees and bowed his head.

After he gave thanks to God on high,

he turned to Lady Bug and said, "Care to fly?"

Lady Bug laughed and danced with glee,

"You're now a bit more like me!"

"You were right all along, God did have a plan.
I was wrong, I'm sorry. Can we still be friends?"
Butterfly smiled and said, "Of course we're still friends!
This is only the start of His plans.

You're still red with black dots; I'm still green with blue.
There's still a big plan for me and you."

So they flew off together, the best of friends; and they knew in their hearts this wasn't the end.

Made in United States
Troutdale, OR
07/10/2023